THE MYSTERY OF...

BIGFOOT

BY
MARY BLOUNT CHRISTIAN

EDITED BY
Dr. Howard Schroeder
Professor in Reading and Language Arts
Dept. of Curriculum and Instruction
Mankato State University

PUBLISHED BY
CRESTWOOD HOUSE
NEW YORK

CIP

LIBRARY OF CONGRESS CATALOGING IN PUBLICATION DATA

Christian, Mary Blount.
  Bigfoot.

  (The Mystery of ——)
  SUMMARY: Provides theories on the hairy beast sighted all over the world and known in North America as Bigfoot or Sasquatch, also suggesting the possibility of its being a hoax.
  1. Sasquatch—Juvenile literature. [1. Sasquatch] I. Schroeder, Howard. II. Title. III. Title: Bigfoot. IV. Series.
QL89.2.S2C47   1987   001.9'44   87-9024
ISBN 0-89686-341-7

International Standard Book Number: 0-89686-341-7	Library of Congress Catalog Card Number: 87-9024

CREDITS

Illustrations:
Cover art: Bob Williams
AP/Wide World Photos: 5, 37
Animals Animals © Michael Dick: 7
International Society of Cryptozoology: 9
Roger Patterson and Bob Gimlin/© Rene Dahinden: 13
UPI/Bettmann Newsphotos: 16, 26, 30, 41
Rene Dahinden: 18, 21, 22, 42
Bob Williams: 24-25, 32-33, 35, 38-39
Fortean Picture Library: 28
Jim Hughes/USDA Forest Service: 44
Andy Schlabach: 46
Graphic Design & Production:
Baker Street Productions, Ltd.

Macmillan Publishing Company
866 Third Avenue
New York, NY 10022
Collier Macmillan Canada, Inc.

CRESTWOOD HOUSE

Printed in the United States of America
10 9 8 7 6 5 4 3 2

BIGFOOT

TABLE OF CONTENTS

Chapter 1

Let your imagination run free for a few moments . . .

You are hiking in the woods when you hear the snap of twigs ahead. Maybe it is a rabbit, or it could be a squirrel. Quietly, so you don't scare the creature, you push aside a bush. You find yourself facing a bear! A big, brown bear!

Your heart thumps loudly in your chest, and you swallow a scream. But the big hairy beast only turns toward you curiously. You stare at it, too scared to run or even turn away. It utters a baby-like cry, then walks slowly away from you.

You let out the breath you've been holding and gasp in more air. With weak legs, you sink to the ground, shaking. You have seen bears at the zoo and in pictures, but never like this one. Wait a minute! There was something different about this bear.

Its face was leathery on the cheeks. Bears have fur all over! And don't bears growl instead of sounding like a baby? And don't bears have dog-like noses? *This* creature had a pug nose and almost no chin. It didn't have paws, you now remember. It had fingers, fingers like a man's fingers!

You listen a moment for a snap, a creak, any hint

Is this Bigfoot?

that the creature might still be near. But you hear nothing. Sure that you are alone, you go to where the beast had stood. There, on the ground, in the dust, is a foot print. Not a paw print. A foot print.

You have just met Bigfoot!

All over the world, people have seen a "man-like" beast with hair all over its body. In Russia, they call it *Almas*. In Tibet, they speak of the *Yeti* or *Abominable Snowman*. Africans call the beast *Chemosit* or *Nandi-*

Bear. In China, there is *Hsing-Hsing.* In North America, it is called *Bigfoot* or *Sasquatch,* the Indian name that means "wild man."

Although descriptions of the "man-beast" vary a bit, it is possible that these beasts are all part of the same general species. Many people find it hard to believe that such a creature can exist. How could it stay so well-hidden from campers and backpackers? Wouldn't we find some remains of its dead? And if Sasquatch were real, wouldn't scientists find some evidence of its existence?

Scientists have sent people to the moon. They have told us great secrets about the universe. But they do not know everything about our planet. Even today, scientists find creatures they had believed were extinct. And they find new creatures they didn't know existed at all.

Australian wallabies (small kangaroos) live in remote England, although few people have seen them or believe they are there. The mountain lion roams from British Columbia to Patagonia, but few are seen or photographed.

Another example is the snow leopard of Asia which was discovered not long ago. For many years, people had told of seeing it. But the snow leopard, or ounce, was thought to be a myth. No bones, no patches of unexplained fur, not even a tooth had been found. Then scientists proved the snow leopard's existence. Why hadn't the experts known before? Why hadn't traces of the snow leopard been found?

Scientists have theories about that mystery. Perhaps

predators carried off and ate the remains. Maybe rain washed them away. We don't know the answers to these questions.

Why, then, are scientists not willing to believe that Bigfoot might be hidden like the snow leopard? Perhaps it is because even the best evidence can't be proven to be true.

Once in a while, the scientists were fooled by the evidence brought to them. When it was proven to be phony, people laughed at them. So now scientists say, "Bring me a Bigfoot; then I will believe it exists."

Believers in Bigfoot point out that, until recently, snow leopards were also thought to be a myth.

Chapter 2

Frank Hansen had a traveling exhibit that he took to small-town fairs. For the price of a ticket, he showed people what he called "The Medieval Man From the Ice Age." Hansen claimed he had found it in a lump of ice in the Bering Straits near Alaska. Another story he told was that he had bought it in Hong Kong from Chinese sailors, who had discovered the block of ice when they were fishing. Other times Hansen said that he had only borrowed the body, and that a rich California movie producer actually owned the creature. With these stories, Hansen began touring the creature on May 3, 1967.

If people had stopped to think, they would have realized that the ice age occurred long before medieval times. When rumors of the exhibit reached scientists, they knew it could not be a medieval man. Still, the "Ice Man" excited them. What if he were an example of a Neanderthal man?

A Belgian scientist, Dr. Bernard Heuvelmans, went to see the "Ice Man" in 1969. He took his rulers, sketchbook, and camera. He peered through the glass coffin. It was difficult to see clearly through the ice. What he saw was a dark body with hair all over, except

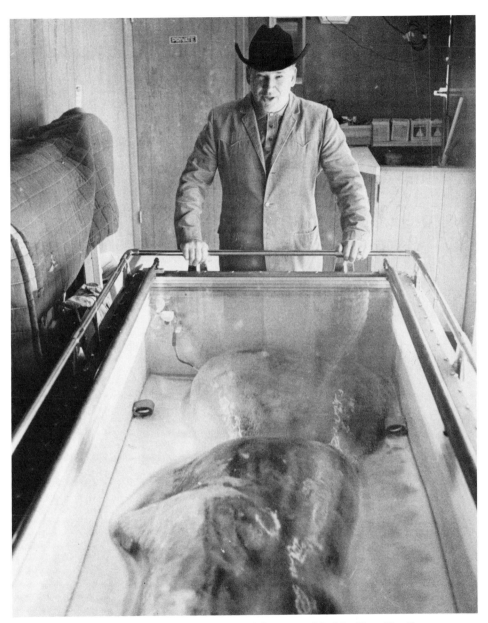

Frank Hansen began touring the United States with his "Ice Man" in 1967.

on its soles, palms and face. The body was extremely large, with features that looked almost human. Dr. Heuvelmans looked closer, his heart pounding with excitement. The creature had been shot!

There were no guns when the Neanderthal man lived. This creature was from *modern* times. Was Dr. Heuvelmans looking at Bigfoot?

The creature had bullet wounds in its face and one forearm. It probably had put up its arm to protect itself. The scientist wanted to examine the creature further, but he didn't get the chance. Frank Hansen and his traveling exhibit seemed to vanish for a while. When he turned up again, there was no "Ice Man."

Later, Dr. Heuvelmans got a letter from the Smithsonian Institute. It said that the creature was just a dummy of latex rubber and hair. Could this expert have been fooled by a dummy?

Heuvelmans does not believe so. He is sure he saw a real body. If it was a real body that had been shot, the police would want to investigate. They might have a murder to deal with. When questioned, Hansen said the creature's real owner, the rich movie producer, was worried about an investigation. The owner came with a refrigerated truck in the night. He took the real body and left the dummy, Hansen claimed.

What was the truth? Was the "Ice Man" real or a hoax? Whichever it was, it is as much a mystery now as it was then.

Chapter 3

Between June, 1964, and December, 1970, there were many reports of "humanoid monsters" in the United States. Most were actual sightings. These incidents occurred in Michigan, Illinois, Wyoming, Ohio, West Virginia, Pennsylvania, Georgia, Alabama, Arizona, Texas, Oklahoma, Missouri, and Wisconsin.

Thousands of huge, human-like tracks have been found as well. Most of them are about seventeen inches (43 cm) long and six inches (15 cm) wide. They have been scattered over 12,500 miles (20,113 km) of "Sasquatch territory," from Alaska to the forests of northern California. Can they *all* be hoaxes?

Some sightings, and even some "evidence," are known hoaxes. For money, attention, or just for the fun of it, people have sometimes pretended to see Bigfoot. Some of these stories can easily be disproved.

Other bits of evidence are not easily discounted, however. In 1967, Roger Patterson and Bob Gimlin were in the woods near Bluff Creek, California, when they saw Bigfoot. They even managed to film the creature.

Patterson was a rancher from Yakima, Washington. Gimlin, who was half Indian, was his guide. Indians from the Yakima Indian Reservation had told Patterson legends about hairy wild men who lived around Mount Saint Helens. Patterson wanted to see them for himself. For years he had looked for Bigfoot every spare moment he had. In 1964, he found fresh Bigfoot tracks. This encouraged him to keep looking for three more years, even though he didn't find any more evidence.

In October, 1967, Patterson and Gimlin were riding their horses, looking for Sasquatch signs on the ground. Suddenly the horses snorted and rolled their eyes. The men spotted a movement about ninety feet (27 m) away. ''Sasquatch,'' Gimlin whispered, his lips barely moving. Patterson and Gimlin stared, almost unable to move.

The creature was female, maybe seven feet (2 m), Patterson later estimated. He thought she was about 350-450 pounds (159-204 kg), although it was hard to guess from that distance. Patterson's horse reared, throwing him to the ground. He quickly scrambled to his feet and grabbed his movie camera from his saddlebag. There was no time to reload the film, adjust the light setting or even to change the focus. He just shot the remaining film in twenty-one seconds.

The faint but unfamiliar clicking of the camera must have caught the creature's attention. She glanced directly at the two men. But she didn't run. And she didn't stop. She just casually strolled into the brush.

Was the creature really a female Bigfoot? Or had one of the local jokesters tried to give the tourists a thrill?

12

In 1967, Roger Patterson and Bob Gimlin took this film of what may have been a female Bigfoot.

Experts from Disney Studios in Hollywood examined the film. Scientists also studied the film in slow motion, fast motion, and one frame at a time. They concluded that it was impossible for a person in an ape suit that big to walk as naturally as the film showed. They estimated that the creature was 280 pounds (127 kg) and about six and a half feet (2 m) tall.

"If it is a hoax," the scientists said, "it is a good one." That was about the best Patterson could hope for from the cautious scientists.

Patterson and Gimlin knew they hadn't faked the film. And they didn't believe they were the victims of a practical joke. When they saw Bigfoot, they had noticed a strong, pungent odor. Other people claiming to have seen Bigfoot had also noticed that smell. And there were footprints, too. Patterson and Gimlin took casts of the prints. These were typical of other Bigfoot prints: larger and wider than a person's, with the big toe separated from the others.

Chapter 4

In January, 1972, Bigfoot was seen near Rowena and the Dalles, Oregon. One cold, dark morning, Deputy Sheriff Harry Gilpin was driving on Highway 80 toward Rowena. The headlights of his patrol car picked up a huge figure crossing the road. The figure climbed a metal fence that divided the highway lanes. Then it disappeared among the trees.

Deputy Gilpin never got a close look at the creature. But the previous June, three men in the area had reported spotting what may have been the same creature. As it was a sunny day, they saw it clearly. The men, owners of a trailer court, had huddled at the window of their office and watched as the creature moved among some rocks. Then it disappeared over a small cliff. Later they agreed that the creature was at least seven feet (2 m) tall and covered with hair.

Deputy Rich Carlson had taken their statements. When he returned to the trailer court that same week, he found that the creature had been seen again.

Their stories attracted Peter Byrne, who helped found the International Wildlife Conservation Society. Byrne used to hunt animals to kill them. But he decided to work to save endangered animals instead.

This Bigfoot track was found by Phil Thompson near Coos Bay, Oregon, in 1976.

16

If this creature was real, it must be endangered, Byrne figured. He and his fellow workers set up a huge telescope that could help them see in the dark. They watched for many months, but they failed to see Bigfoot even once in Oregon.

Byrne had more work ahead, though. Near Estacada, Oregon, a man saw a Bigfoot father, mother, and child digging in a rock pile. Other sightings were made near Willard, Washington, and near the Columbia River near Stevenson. In addition, prints were found near Mount Adams.

Another important sighting happened in Deltox Marsh near Fremont, Wisconsin, in November, 1966. Six young men were in the marsh, making noise to drive wild deer from hiding. Imagine their surprise when, instead of deer, they drove out a large, powerfully built creature with short, dark hair! It stood on two legs and had a hairy chest and long arms. It ambled out of the woods, showing no fear of the six young hunters. Instead, it seemed interested in them.

"Inquisitive" is a word people often use to describe the creature. It means "very curious about the actions of others." One man claimed he was chased by Bigfoot. When he took off his boot and threw it at the creature, the "man-beast" forgot about the chase and sat down to examine the boot! Bigfoot has been known to carry off unusual objects, such as tents, rubber rafts, and even a bedroll—with a man still in it!

In 1971, Richard Brown saw a Bigfoot while hunting in Oregon. Here, he stands near the site.

18

Bigfoot has also been seen in Michigan. Two years before the Wisconsin incident, from June 14 to July 6, 1964, *The Sunday Express* in Sisters Lake carried stories about strange sightings nearby:

• Strawberry pickers fled from the fields in terror. They were frightened by a huge "shaggy gorilla or bear" which they said was nine feet (2.7 m) tall.

• Gordon Brown from Georgia, his wife, and two friends had been driving a lonely stretch of road near Sisters Lake. Suddenly the car's headlights revealed a huge creature crossing the road. At first they thought it was a bear. But it walked on two feet, like a man. When it disappeared into the woods, Brown and the others started to follow it. But they became afraid and turned back when their flashlight batteries went dead.

• A woman from a nearby farm said she wasn't surprised at the news. She said something had been coming around at night, causing the farm animals to bellow in terror.

The newspaper articles soon attracted Bigfoot hunters to Sisters Lake. Gun-toting strangers were everywhere, it seemed. Soon the sheriff said enough was enough. He sent everyone home before they started to shoot anything that moved. Gradually, the stories stopped. But did they stop because the sightings stopped? Or was it because the community was too embarrassed to say anything more?

Chapter 5

Although most Bigfoot sightings have occurred since the 1950's, it's possible that the creature has been seen as early as the 1920's.

One story tells of Albert Ostman, who was prospecting for gold in Toba Inlet, British Columbia, in 1924. Indians had told him that other people had gone into the woods, never to return. The *Sosskwatl* had killed them, the Indians warned. But Ostman wasn't scared. He went into the woods, anyway.

Food was stolen from Ostman's campsite, but he stayed on. One night, he was shaken awake. Something was carrying him—and he was still inside his sleeping bag! At last, he was set down. He crawled slowly from his sleeping bag—and found himself face-to-face with a Bigfoot family! He said the female seemed upset that the male had brought home such a creature.

Ostman said that the Sasquatch did not try to harm him. Instead, they watched curiously as he cooked his food. When Ostman offered the male some tobacco, Bigfoot swallowed it and became sick. During the confusion, Ostman escaped.

The man didn't tell anyone about his adventure until he heard of other Bigfoot adventures. He had been afraid no one would believe him.

Another famous Bigfoot incident also happened in 1924. Five miners were staying in a cabin in the woods east of Mount Saint Helens, Washington, while they panned for gold. They began finding big footprints around their camp. And several times they saw something that looked like a huge ape.

Eventually, one of the miners spotted the huge creature at the edge of a canyon. The miner shot it in the back. The creature fell into the canyon, and its body was swept away by a swift mountain stream.

That night, the miners cringed in terror while rocks

Albert Ostman claims to have been carried off by a Bigfoot in 1924—while he was in his sleeping bag!

were pelted at their cabin. Screeches and howls filled the air. The men poked their rifles through small holes in their cabin walls and fired into the night. But the attack continued until dawn. As soon as the men dared, they fled back to civilization.

After they told their story to a newspaper, a search party went back to the camp to investigate. The party found the wrecked cabin and huge boulders thrown about. They also found big footprints and tufts of black hair. Ever since this incident, the area has been known as "Ape Canyon."

Fred Beck shows the rifle he used in the 1924 "Ape Canyon" incident to Rene Dahinden.

Chapter 6

The United States isn't the only country claiming to have "man-like beasts." Such creatures have also been seen in Tibet, India, Russia, and China.

During the 1950's, there were sightings in Asia of a creature known as "Yeti." In the Himalayan mountains, pilgrims on their way to religious shrines told of seeing "a race of giant men" in the mountains and unexplored areas. People at monasteries in Tibet spoke of unknown "wild men."

A legend in Tibet says that its people are descended from the "Monkey King and a female creature that dwelled among the rocks." Many of the lamas (holy men) from Tibet have high, domed heads, which is one feature of the Yeti.

Over the years, three types of Yeti have been described. One is large and docile. Another is a savage, muscular meat-eater, five feet tall (1.5 m) and hairy. The third is like a "little man," shy and shaggy.

Ancient Tibetan medical books describe folk medicine made from the Yeti's fat, gall and blood. The books show animals that are familiar to us, but they also show the Yeti, standing on two feet. Perhaps the Yeti once was plentiful, before it was hunted for its medicinal uses.

This illustration shows the areas of the world where sightings of "man-beasts" have been made.

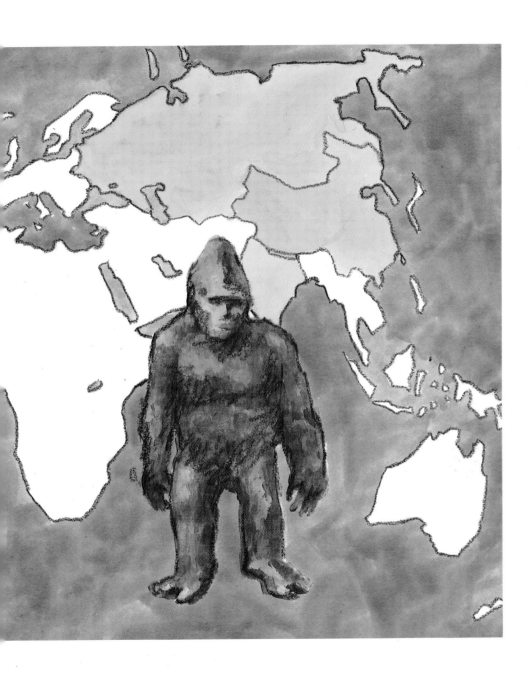

In the Tibetan monasteries, lamas beat huge gongs to scare the Yeti away. But they have shown Yeti scalps to visitors. They say that the scalps have been in the temple for more than three hundred years. The scalps are still used in religious ceremonies. The lamas also have the remains of a hand, which they said belonged to a Yeti.

In 1960, Sir Edmund Hillary brought one of the Yeti scalps out of Tibet for testing. Experts said it was a phony made from the skin of a scrow, which is a Himalayan mountain goat. Disappointed, Sir Hillary threw the relic aside and eventually lost it. Maybe there

Sir Edmund Hillary, left, watches his Nepalese guide display a scalp which, according to Tibetan monks, may be from a Yeti.

never was a real scalp. Or maybe the lamas didn't want a sacred scalp leaving the temple. Whatever the truth, this incident helped to convince people that creatures like Yeti and Bigfoot were only myths.

But what about the earlier incidents? Colonel C.K. Howard-Bury led an expedition up Mount Everest in 1921. He found footprints that he said were three times the size of a human foot. The native guides said the prints were those of the *Metch-Kangmi. Kang* means *snow* in Tibet. *Mi* means *man. Metch* means *disgusting* or *ragged.* It was misinterpreted as abominable, so the creature became known as the Abominable Snowman, "cousin" to Bigfoot.

There have been many expeditions to look for the Yeti or Metch-Kangmi. English climber Eric Shipton found and photographed footprints in 1951. Tom Slick, a Texas businessman, discovered additional footprints that were ten and thirteen inches (25 and 33 cm) long. Neither man made an actual sighting.

In India, the man-beast is called *Rakshi* or *Rakshasa.* It is mentioned in one of India's national epics, *Rama and Sita,* written by a poet in the third or fourth century B.C. A travel book about the Himalayas, published in 1820, refers to unidentified tracks, too.

Unlike the American Bigfoot and the Yeti, the Russian Bigfoot is known as a nuisance and a prankster. The *Almas* is said to be very large. It sometimes raids vegetable gardens for food.

For a long time, Russian scientists were forbidden

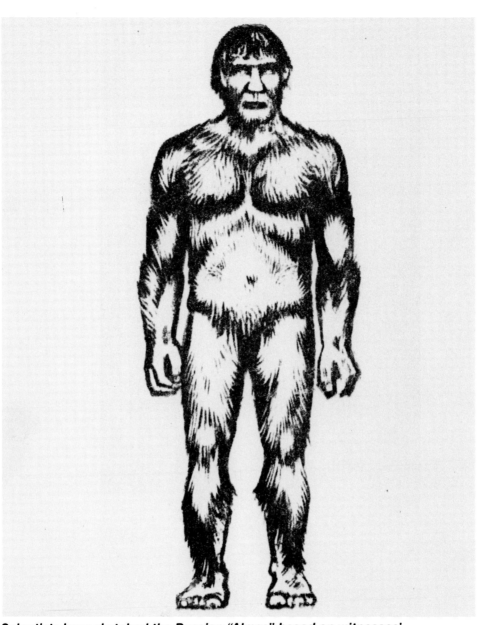

Scientists have sketched the Russian "Almas" based on witnesses' descriptions.

to mention the Almas. Now they have permission to study the creature. Russian scientists used an *identikit* to draw the Almas from witnesses' descriptions. The system is similar to that used by police. From the descriptions given the scientists, they drew the likeness of an animal much like Bigfoot.

The Russian goal is not to catch the Almas but to photograph it. The scientists are trying to get a head count. Once they know how many Almas there are, the scientists want to "domesticate" them and set up a reserve. There the Almas will be protected from the people.

Almas are said to live in dense mountains, forests, and gorges below the snow line. The scientists say it eats plants, grasses, berries, roots, insects, and small animals. It leaves a footprint about twelve and a half inches (32 cm) long and six and a half inches (16.5 cm) wide, with the thick big toe and second toe separate from the others. The print is similar to the prints of the first Stone Age man, Neanderthal, whose skeleton and footprints lay undisturbed in Italian caves until 1952.

A.G. Pronin is a hydrologist, a scientist devoted to the study of water. In August, 1958, Mr. Pronin was looking for a campsite at the edge of the Fedchenko Glacier in Russia. Three times he spotted large, hairy creatures watching him. They didn't come close to him, though, so he wasn't bothered. When the rest of his crew arrived, they must have scared the creatures away with their noise. The creatures weren't seen again. But

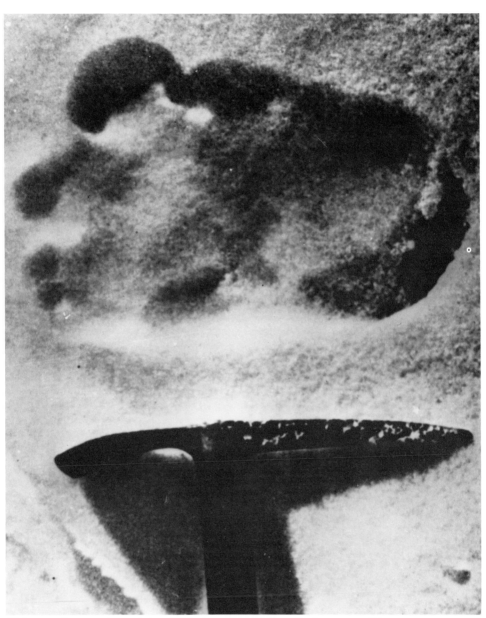

This track was found in 1958 by mountain climbers on Mount Everest. Is this the footprint of a Bigfoot?

when Pronin and his men were ready to leave, they couldn't find the rubber raft. They thought it had broken loose, so they searched for it downstream. Failing to find it, they left.

Several weeks later, peasants found the raft wedged between rocks on top of a mountain. "It would have had to go against the rapids and over the shoals and uphill," Pronin said, puzzled.

The peasants told him "the being likes to be impudent." They explained that the Almas often took clothes and cooking utensils, dropping them miles away.

Are these creatures really this bold, or only curious? They may not have the thinking process involved with having a sense of humor. In fact, their thinking process may not be well-developed at all. In 1927, a caravan in Mongolia was left unattended for a time. When the people returned, they found Almas warming themselves by a dying fire. There was plenty of kindling, but the creatures did not seem to know how to throw it onto the fire.

Also, the Almas had eaten dates and sweets they had found in saddlebags. But the rest of the food was in jars. The Almas didn't seem to know how to remove the lids or even break the glass to get at the food.

The same holds true for Bigfoot. In the United States, there is no evidence that Bigfoot cooks food, has articulate speech, or has used even the most simple of tools.

Current maps of China show the "Hsing-Hsing Hsia," translated as "Ravine of Stars." Gordon W.

Creighton, an expert on geographic names, thought "Ravine of Stars" sounded odd. He wondered about the origin of the name.

Creighton consulted a dictionary compiled in the eighteenth century for the Manchur Emperor K'ang Hsi. It said Hsing Hsing meant "great ape," with a "face of a dog and the build of a man. Its cry is like the wailing of a small child."

In 1954, Pai Hsin, a director of films for the Chinese People's Army, was trying to find a good location for a movie set. Roaming about an isolated area of China, he saw what he thought were two people in the distance.

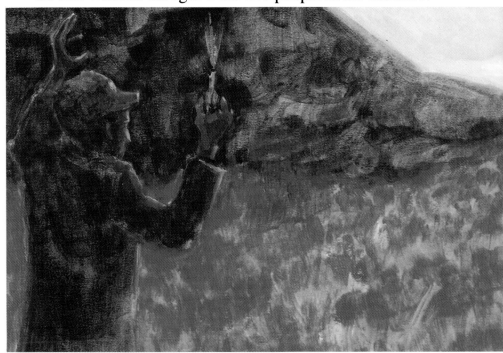

This illustration shows what Pai Hsin saw in 1954.

He waved and shot his pistol into the air to get their attention. But they didn't even look up, he said.

Later, he saw them again among some rocks. But when he tried to climb up to them, they easily scampered away from him. Pai Hsin soon realized that these were not ordinary people. They walked like men, but they were hairy all over.

Another time, near Mount Muztagh Atu in Pamus, Army guards noticed their meat was spoiled. They threw it outside the cabin. "Wild men" then picked it up and ran away with it, the guards claimed.

Chapter 7

Since the early 1900's, there have been ten reported cases of captured man-beasts. Yet not a single skeleton or stuffed skin has been saved for proof. Were the captures real, or were they hoaxes?

In 1910, in Kazakh, Central Asia, two men spotted a figure they thought was a horse thief. Yelling, they chased after it. It ran awkwardly and not very fast. When lassoed, it "squeaked like a hare."

One of the men realized it was just a "harmless wild man" and not a thief. It was male, short, and covered with thick, reddish hair, they said. Its long arms reached to below the knees, and its shoulders were stooped. Its brow sloped and jutted above the eyes. Although it had large ears, it had no ear lobes. Its feet were one and a half times broader than a human's, with the big toe shorter and set apart from the other toes.

The men let the creature go, and it hurried off into the night. Curious, the men followed it to a hollowed-out spot below an overhanging cliff. They saw dried grass thrown about the spot. The man who had seen the beasts before said they were usually in pairs and were harmless.

Later that year, a female was captured. She slept with

her knees and elbows beneath her body. Her forehead rested on the ground, and she kept her hands at the back of her neck during sleep. Her captors used her for farm work but later released her. She ran off into the brush.

In northern India, in 1950, Mira Behn began researching the man-like creatures. She asked local herdsmen about the creatures in the area. At first they denied ever having seen any. Finally, they admitted they had tracked and killed a creature that had stolen a local woman. Because they considered the creature a ''hairy man,'' they didn't report the incident. They were afraid they would be charged with murder.

A "wild man" with thick, reddish hair was mistaken for a horse thief by two men in Kazakh, Central Asia, in 1910.

35

Chapter 8

The man-like creatures have been seen in both Asia and North America, and there may be a good reason for that. Many thousands of years ago, Asia and Alaska were connected by a land bridge. The bridge was one hundred miles (161 km) wide. Herds of animals migrated across the bridge from Asia to North America, looking for food. Perhaps it was then that the first of the man-like beasts crossed over.

Perhaps some stayed behind. Is that why the creatures seen on both continents are similar? There seem to be as many varieties of Bigfoot as there are of man. The Yeti is a "beast-like man." The Bigfoot is a "man-like beast."

The Yeti has left footprints at altitudes of 12,000 to 25,000 feet (3,658-7,620 m) above the snow line. However, most of its prints have been found around altitudes of fifteen thousand feet (4,572 m). Some believe the Yeti lives above the snow line and comes down in search of food. Others think it would be impossible for a creature of that size to live so high up all the time.

The Yeti is noted for his strong smell and high-pitched, whistling or mewing call. Bigfoot emits an odor and makes a soft cry, too. The Bigfoot is much taller,

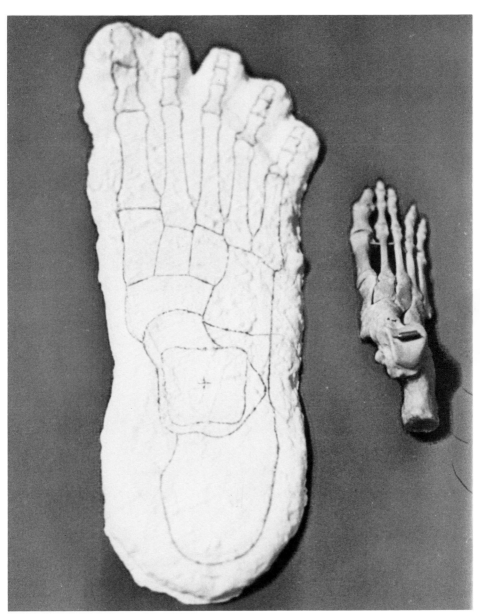

This photo compares a human foot with the foot of Sasquatch.

This illustration shows a cross-section of the Himalayan Mountains and the altitudes where tracks of the Yeti have been seen.

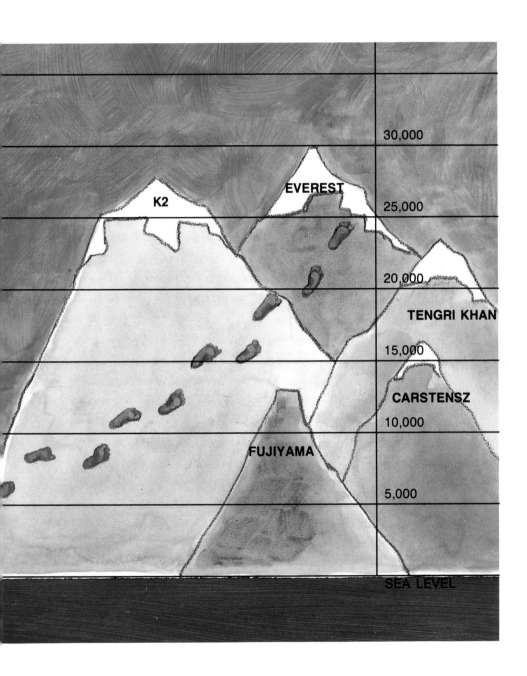

30,000

EVEREST

K2

25,000

20,000

TENGRI KHAN

15,000

CARSTENSZ

10,000

FUJIYAMA

5,000

SEA LEVEL

39

however. Reported heights are seven to ten feet (2-3 m), with some weights estimated at more than five hundred pounds (227 kg). The smaller Sasquatch are believed to be females or young ones. Bigfoot has been seen eating berries, fruit, leaves, spruce tips, water plants, tubers, fish, and rodents. Some witnesses say it also eats deer, sheep, cows, and horses, although these were probably killed by a bear and not by Bigfoot.

Like the Yeti, the Russian Almas seem to have three types. The very large one is vegetarian, unless it is very hungry. The medium-size Almas is more aggressive and is a meat-eating hunter. The smallest type of Almas, which the peasants called *Rakshi Bompo,* is mischievous, raiding crops and running away when discovered.

Bigfoot is described as having a receding forehead and chin, a broad chest, short legs and long arms. Bigfoot has been seen during every month of the year. The creature does not seem to hibernate. Primates do not hibernate.

Another thing people have noticed about Bigfoot is its "eye shine." Nocturnal (night-prowling) animals have eyes that help them see better at night. Their eyes reflect the available light, which then bounces back through the pupil.

The eyes of nocturnal animals give off a green reflection. Diurnal (day-prowling) animals give off a red, pale pink or white reflection. Bigfoot is said to reflect red, yellow, green, and white. This means that no one can say for sure if Bigfoot is nocturnal or diurnal.

Soviet expedition member Igor Burtsev compares his own foot with the plaster cast of a print thought to belong to the Abominable Snowman.

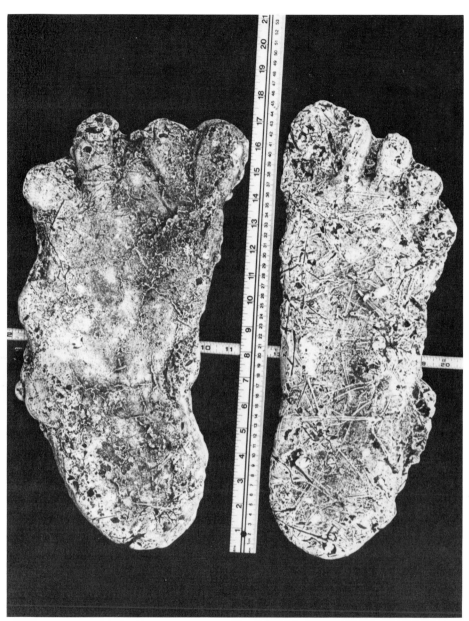

Shown above are casts of the famous Bossburg prints. Notice the "club" foot on the left.

42

All over the world, residents, geologists, travelers, and sportsmen have found a large number of tracks in snow, sand, and mud. They've taken pictures, done sketches, and made plaster casts of the footprints. This has given scientists information about how Bigfoot may walk.

Many animals can walk on two legs for a while. But it is the way in which the foot moves the body forward that makes people different from animals. A normal human lands on the outer side of the foot and takes off from the inner side. The Sasquatch lands on the inner border and takes off from the outer one, with its toes pointed slightly inward.

However, two very different Sasquatch prints have been found. One is the "hour glass" with the big and second toes separated—but the same size—as the little toes. This creature walks with the main weight on the inside of the foot.

A more human-type print was found in Washington State. It is called the Bossburg print. This creature had one normal foot and one clubbed foot. The left foot was similar in every way to that of a human, except for its size. It was seventeen and a half inches (44 cm) long and seven inches (18 cm) wide! The right foot had been injured, probably in the creature's youth, and didn't heal well.

Which set of prints is real? Are they both real? Or are they both fake?

If they both are real, we must have two kinds of Big-

If Bigfoot is to be found, it will probably be in remote areas like this.

foot. If they both are fake, someone has gone to a lot of trouble—over a period of many years—to play a joke on us.

Maybe the man-beast is some creature from our past that has survived in isolated areas. As modern man closes in, taking more and more wilderness for his own, Bigfoot must go deeper into hiding. Fewer sightings are reported as time passes. Is Bigfoot getting better at staying away from people? Or is Bigfoot dying out?

Is Bigfoot an endangered species? If so, should it be protected like other endangered species?

Whatever the answer, people continue to be interested in the large, hairy man-beasts that have been seen on two continents over the past century.

Map

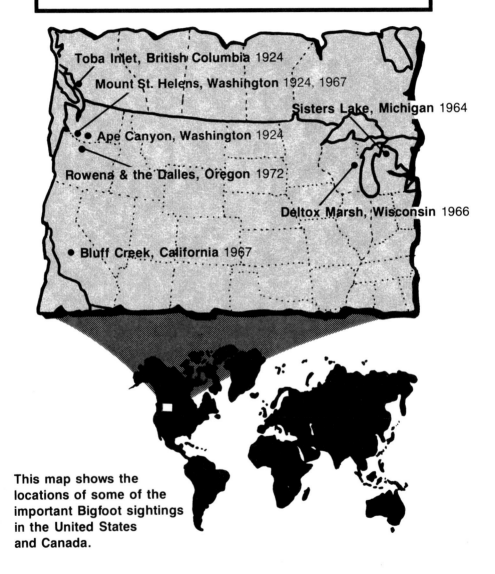

Toba Inlet, British Columbia 1924

Mount St. Helens, Washington 1924, 1967

Sisters Lake, Michigan 1964

Ape Canyon, Washington 1924

Rowena & the Dalles, Oregon 1972

Deltox Marsh, Wisconsin 1966

Bluff Creek, California 1967

This map shows the
locations of some of the
important Bigfoot sightings
in the United States
and Canada.

Glossary/Index